Happy,

Ken Stephenson

HOW TO EXPLAIN THE TRINITY

HOW TO EXPLAIN
THE TRINITY TO YOUR CHILD
USING A PUPPET STAGE

Kenneth D. Stephenson

This book is dedicated to the work, ministry, and memory of the late Dr. Henry M. Morris, whose writings in his book *Science and the Bible* inspired the writing of this book.

ABOUT THE AUTHOR

Ken Stephenson was born in Manhattan, Kansas in 1949 to Wallace and Patricia Stephenson, and grew up in Leigh and Papillion, Nebraska. After graduating with a Bachelors Degree in zoology from Nebraska University in 1972, he served as the communications officer aboard the U.S.S. Windham County, and was then shore based for fourteen months in Yokosuka, Japan. It was in a Japanese apartment in Yokosuka, Japan that Ken came to know Jesus Christ as his Lord and Savior.

A few days after he became a Christian, Ken remembers asking the Lord the question, "Lord, what about the Trinity? Is it even an important question? Does it even matter if the Trinity is true or not?"

After an honorable discharge from the United States Navy, Ken attended Manhattan Christian College in Manhattan, Kansas and majored in missions.

Then in 1987, long after Ken had forgotten he had asked his Lord the Trinity question, the Lord gave him the answer. It came while reading Dr. Henry Morris' book *Science and the Bible*.

The book in your hand is the compilation of more than two decades of Bible study, prayer, and meditation on the divine nature of the God of the Bible.

Ken invites you to join him in the pursuit of the living God.

TABLE OF CONTENTS

INTRODUCTION

Since the beginning of time the spirit of man has been on a quest to understand God's divine nature. A few of us, for example Moses on Mount Sinai, have had a close encounter with the God of creation and have lived to tell their story. Yet, when a boy asks his father, "What is God like?" most of us are still without an adequate answer.

Since the coming of Jesus of Nazareth hundreds of Christian scholars have written eloquently about the God of the Bible and His divine nature. Many of them have demonstrated conclusively from the scriptures that the Father is God, that the Son (Jesus) is God, and that the Holy Spirit is God, but yet the Church has fallen short of actually explaining logically how this can be so. The critics of Christianity- and they are many- say that since Christianity is founded on a completely illogical doctrinal foundation that Christianity is itself illogical.

But take heart Christian! What you have believed by faith is indeed true. You are about to see that the Trinity is not only true, but it is unquestionably the most logical explanation of the essence of God's divine nature, and why He created the universe the way He did. Not only is it true, but it can be <u>clearly seen</u>, and <u>understood</u> with man's finite mind.

When was the last time you heard a sermon at church entitled "How to Explain the Trinity"? For nearly all of us, the answer to that question is "never," and rightfully so. I would not try to explain to you how to fix an automobile engine. I don't UNDERSTAND how to fix an automobile engine. Although I KNOW the engine works, I really don't know "how" it works. Similarly, the Christian knows in his "knower" that the Father is God, the Son is God, and the Holy Spirit is God, and that there is just one God, but he doesn't know how to explain that to you ... until now.

For those of you who picked up this book truly seeking to know God, I want you to know that we have ALL fallen short, and we are ALL in need of a Savior. That Savior is Jesus, and if you would like to know him as your Lord and Savior, there is a prayer to help you come to know Him in the back section of this book.

I pray that you enjoy the experience of understanding the Trinity as much as I have. Indeed, just like the Apostle Paul said in Ephesians 1:17, "I keep asking that the God of our Lord Jesus Christ, the glorious Father, may give you the Spirit of wisdom and revelation, so that you may know him better."

Chapter I

How to Explain the Trinity: The Explanation Authorized by Scripture

The Christian doctrine of the Trinity has been commonly referred to as a "mystery." How God can be Father, Son, and Holy Spirit, and yet be just one God can seem like nonsense to a non-Christian, and Christians have said they just "believe it by faith." Although God honors the faith of the Christian, there is a perfectly logical way to explain the doctrine of the Trinity from scripture, and it can be CLEARLY SEEN, and UNDERSTOOD.

Before teaching you how to explain the Trinity we need to define it. Stated simply, the God of the Bible is one God in three persons, the Father, the Son, and the Holy Spirit. It is easy to show from scripture that the *Father is God* (Isaiah 63:15-16; Matthew 6:9; John 17:1-3), the *Son is God* (Isaiah 9:6; John 8:58; John 10:30-33; John 20:27-28; Titus 2:13), and the *Holy Spirit is God* (Job 33:4; Psalms 139:7-8; Acts 5:3-4; 1 Corinthians 2:10-11; 2 Corinthians 3:17-18), and yet *there is just one God* (Deuteronomy 6:4; Mark 12:29; Romans 3:30; 1 Timothy 1:17), but the challenge has always been to make sense out of that. By what law of logic does 1 + 1 + 1 = 1? It doesn't. It equals three. Is the Christian doctrine of the Trinity nonsense or is it logically sound?

It is an inescapable truth that while on this earth man's finite mind will never be able to fully comprehend the depths of God. Man's understanding of who God is and what He is like (what His divine nature is like) is totally dependent on what God CHOOSES to reveal about Himself. The important question is, "Has God chosen to reveal to us what His divine nature is like?" The answer is YES!

In ***Romans 1:19-20*** we read the following from the New International Version (NIV) of the Scriptures: "Since what may be ***known*** about God is plain to them, because God has made it plain to them. v. 20 For **since the creation of the world** God's invisible qualities – his eternal power and ***divine nature*** – have been ***clearly seen***, being ***understood*** from what has been made, so that men are without excuse." Notice in verse 19 that there is something man can **KNOW** about God. We don't have to guess or speculate; we can KNOW it. Romans 1:20 tells us that if we go back to the point in time at which the world was created (Genesis 1:1) and behold the things that God created then, we ought to be able to ***CLEARLY SEE***, and we ought to be able to ***UNDERSTAND*** the divine nature of God.

So to understand whether God is a Trinity or not, let's go back to the point in time at which the world was created, Genesis 1:1, and find out what God created then that CAUSED His divine nature to be CLEARLY SEEABLE and UNDERSTANDABLE. Remember, what God's divine nature is like ought to be so obvious that MEN ARE WITHOUT EXCUSE not to see it (see the end of Romans 1:20).

In Genesis 1:1 there were three "components" of the universe "spoken into existence" by the Creator, and none of these three components had any prior existence. Those three things were:

1) ***TIME***: "The beginning" is when time began. See 2Timothy 1:9. Time as we know it had a very definite beginning point and that was the awesome moment of Genesis 1:1.

2) ***SPACE***: The word "heavens" in Genesis 1:1 is referring to the expanse of the heavens, or space (See Isaiah 40:22). The word "heavens" in Isaiah 40:22 is the same Hebrew word used for "heavens" in Genesis 1:1. The word "heavens" can

also refer to the sun, moon, and stars but they were all created on the fourth day of the creation week (Genesis 1:16).

3) *MATTER*: The earth is matter, or the elements. Matter includes solids, liquids, gases, light, and energy. Matter was created and became visible in the first moment of time. Hebrews 11:3 makes it obvious that matter had a definite beginning.

There are three very important physical characteristics of **TIME, SPACE,** and **MATTER** that we need to keep in mind. They are:

1) None of the three can be either *created or destroyed* by man. You can say you have "made time" to do something, but you haven't "made" anything. You just stopped doing one thing and started doing another. Time ticks on at exactly the same speed regardless of how we perceive it. Consider one cubic foot of space in front of you. You can't cancel it, you can't burn it, and you can't blow it up. It's just "there," and there is nothing you can do to change it. One of the laws of science we all learned in high school, the first law of thermodynamics, states that "matter can neither be created nor destroyed." You can burn a log and "change the form" of the log from wood to heat, energy, and ash, but the total amount of matter and energy remains the same.

2: If any one of the three were to *cease to exist*, the entire creation would also cease to exist. The creation is totally dependent on the existence of all three for its existence to be *experienced* and *meaningful*. If time were to "cease to exist," there could be no experience of any kind. If space ceased to exist there would be no "place" for matter to exist. If matter ceased to exist nothing would matter anyway, because there would be "nothing" here. So to have a meaningful and experience-able creation, you *must* have time, space, and matter.

3. The creation is *not* part time, part space, and part matter. Rather, it is 100 percent time (time is everywhere, i.e. there is no place that time isn't present), 100 percent space, (space is everywhere, i.e. there is no place where space isn't present),

and 100 percent matter, (when matter is considered to be solids, liquids, gasses, *light*, and energy).

Now, keep in mind that Romans 1:20 *authorizes the following analogy*:

God the Father is analogous to space. Both space and God the Father are omnipresent (everywhere at one time), and both space and God the Father are *invisible*. John 1:18 says, "No one has ever seen God, but God the One and Only (Jesus), who is at the Father's side, has made him known". No one has *ever* seen God the Father, just like no one has *ever* seen space (see 1 Timothy 6:16). When you open your eyes and try to "see," all you can see is matter *in* space, but you can't see space.

God the Son is analogous to matter. Jesus was real matter that we could see, touch, and talk to. And when He died on the cross, He bled *real* blood. We are literally *saved* by *real* matter, the blood of Jesus, the Son. *Anytime* anyone in scripture had an encounter with God, and God actually appeared in a seeable form, they were seeing a manifestation of Jesus, the Son.

Notice that after the resurrection of Jesus He still had a body of flesh and bones (matter) (see Luke 24:39) and He could choose to be in a visible form (Luke 24:39) or an invisible form (Luke 24:30-31) just like there are visible (solids) and invisible (some gases) forms of matter.

God the Holy Spirit is analogous to time. Time is the continuum over which you and I *experience* space and matter. If time were to stop, even if you were real, I couldn't experience you. Likewise, God the Holy Spirit makes it possible for you and me to *experience* the Father and the Son. Take away the Holy Spirit, and what you have left is a *religion*, not a *relationship* with the living God. It is not until the Holy Spirit moves upon your spirit in the born again experience (see the gospel of John, Chapter 3), that you can *know* the Father and the Son in a personal way. Until then, all you have is a religion.

Now, here comes the revelation of the Trinity. What God created in Genesis 1:1 was 100 percent time, 100 percent space, and 100 percent matter simultaneously! It (the creation) is simultaneously all of each of the three all at one time and the three are totally inseparable. You can *not* take time out of space and matter. You can *not* take matter out of space and time, and you can *not* take space out of time and matter. This should tell us something about the divine nature of God! (Read Romans 1:20 again). **God is 100 percent Father, 100 percent Son**, and **100 percent Holy Spirit** *simultaneously,* just like what He has made is 100 percent space, 100 percent matter, and 100 percent time simultaneously! And the Father, the Son, and the Holy Spirit can not be separated. Take just a moment for that to sink in. If you "catch it" (if the Lord reveals it to you) you will "own" God's divine nature, and it will be <u>seeable</u> and <u>understandable</u>.

Hold your hand in front of your face. Your hand is 100 percent matter, it is 100 percent filled with space (or exists in space), and it exists 100 percent in time, and there is *nothing* you can do to change that. Consider a 12" X 12" X 12" area of space in front of you. That area of space is 100 percent filled with matter (matter in the form of gases in the air and light), and it is 100 percent filled with time. Can you "clearly see" God's divine nature, understanding it by what has been made? (Romans 1:20).

Since Romans 1:20 says that God's divine nature can be clearly seen and understood (comprehended with man's finite mind), it would follow logically that if God is 100 percent Father, 100 percent Son, and 100 percent Holy Spirit simultaneously, then they would each have to be omnipresent (everywhere at one time) just like time, space, and matter are omnipresent.

Does this agree with scripture? Absolutely! That God the Father is omnipresent can be seen in Jeremiah 23:24 where it says "do not **I** fill heaven and earth declares the Lord?" Since the Father, Son, and Holy spirit are not separable, just like space, matter, and time are not separable, it could be argued that the word "Lord" in Jeremiah 23:24 is referring to all three. But for the sake of this discussion, let's assume that the verse is referring to God the Father.

That God the Holy Spirit is omnipresent can be seen in Psalms 139:7-10, which makes it obvious that man can not hide from the Holy Spirit.

That God the Son is omnipresent may at first seem less obvious, but it can definitely be demonstrated that He is. When you read that matter is *everywhere* you had to stop and think for a moment before you realized that unseen gases and light were also matter, which makes matter omnipresent. So it can be shown that the Son is omnipresent and able to be in a seeable or unseen form at will. The following are some of the scriptures that show the Son's omnipresence:

1. Matthew 18:20: "For where two or three come together in my name, there am I with them." There could be millions of such gatherings in the world at any one time, most (if not all) of which the Son would be in an unseen form.
2. Matthew 28:20b: "And surely I am with you always, to the very end of the Age". If Jesus is with Christians always, omnipresence must be one of his attributes.
3. Ephesians 1:23: "the church which is His body, the fullness of him who fills everything in every way."
4. Ephesians 4:1: "He who descended is the very one who ascended higher than all the heavens, in order to fill the whole universe."
5. Colossians 3:11c: "but Christ is all, and is in all."
6. John 10:30: "I and the Father are one." In this verse Jesus says He and the Father are one, thus claiming to be God, which is obvious by the words of His listeners (see John 10:31-33). Although it is surely true that Jesus and the Father are one in a spiritual sense, you now understand it is also true in a physical sense. If the Father and Jesus are one as space and matter are one (the analogy to understand God's divine nature authorized by Romans 1:20), and the Father is omnipresent, then the Son is also omnipresent.
7. John 10:38b: "that you may *know* and understand that the Father is in me and I in the Father". If Jesus is in the Father, and the Father is omnipresent, then Jesus is omnipresent.

Notice that time, space, and matter are three distinct entities, and each has its own _function_ in the creation. Time is not space or matter, but time makes experiencing space and matter possible. Space is not time or matter, but space makes a "place" for matter and time to exist. Matter is not time or space, but matter gives the creation substance and meaning.

Although time, space, and matter continuously interrelate one with the others, they are totally and completely *inseparable*. This perfectly describes the nature of God.

As a Christian, I have a great respect for the written word (logos). Each word has a *great* significance. That being said- and this is of utmost importance- we can "say the words" space and matter and time as if one of the three can exist only by itself and not be permeated by the other two, but in reality this is just an illusion. You cannot, by definition, have an area of space that is not *simultaneously* filled *completely* with time and matter, or a portion of matter that is not *simultaneously* filled *completely* with space and time, or a "unit" of time in which space and matter does not exist.

The exact same principles apply to the Father, Son, and Holy Spirit. We can say the "word" Father and our minds can imagine the Father existing as a "separate" entity, but in the exact same way that space is TOTALLY filled with matter and time, The Father is *totally filled* with the Son and the Holy Spirit. In John 10:30 Jesus says, "I and the Father are one." In John 17:21 (and in John 10:38; 14:10; 14:11 and 14:20) Jesus says, "Father, just as *you are in me and I am in you*."

Can you now see that if we are going to attempt to equate God's divine nature to a mathematical equation (and that could be said to be absurd to begin with) it would not be $1 + 1 + 1$, but rather $1 \times 1 \times 1 = 1$? That represents a perfect Trinity of the ONE God of the Bible.

It is interesting that each of the three of time, space, and matter are also a miniature model of the Trinity. Time is past, present, and future, each of which is the totality of time. Space is height, width, and depth. If you just have height and width, but no depth, you still have nothing. It isn't until you add the third dimension of depth that you have anything *real* and *experiencable*. Matter is solids, liquids, and gases.

For you scientists who are reading this, let's consider the scientific law of cause and effect. That law would cause us to predict that the nature of the effect (the universe) ought to be a duplicate of the nature of its cause (God). That is, the divine nature of God ought to be reflected in what He has made. This is exactly what we have found. It is *perfectly* reflected in what He has made, and it has been right in front of your nose your entire life. So, you are indeed "without excuse" (see the end of Romans 1:20).

So what God made in Genesis 1:1 is a *perfect trinity* of space, matter, and time, just like God is a *perfect Trinity* of Father, Son, and Holy Spirit.

I do not pretend to be a Greek or Hebrew scholar. I do not pretend to have all the answers or the final say in how to explain the Trinity. It occurs to me that "seeing" how to explain what God's divine nature is like answers some questions, and opens up a million *new* questions. So if you have questions, comments, or corrections e-mail me at Godisatrinity1@live.com

Amen. Come Lord Jesus.

CHAPTER 2

THE THROUGH THE BIBLE TRINITY BIBLE STUDY

One of two things must be true. Either the time, space, matter analogy presented in Chapter 1 as *the* way to explain what God's divine nature is like (is He a Trinity, or is He not a Trinity?) is erroneous and a terrible misapplication of the truth presented in the scriptures, or it is one of the most beautiful divine revelations ever given to mankind. One that not only explains to the finite mind what the God of the bible is like, but makes God's physical nature as obvious as the nose on your face. One would expect that if the revelation is indeed true you would "see" that truth all throughout the scriptures. It should be affirmed over and over again in ways that would confirm it to our hearts.

It is my honest opinion that we do indeed see that affirmation all throughout scripture.

In this chapter, we are going to explore the amazing depths of the Trinity (divine nature of God) throughout the Bible, with emphasis on authenticating the time, space, matter analogy authorized by Romans 1:20. If you haven't yet read *and understood* Chapter 1 or Chapter 3 of this book before starting this Bible study, I highly recommend that you do so. It will greatly increase your understanding during this Bible study.

The scriptures selected are numbered 1 through 60 in this chapter, and I have selected 30 scriptures as key *verses*. The key *verses* are the scriptures I feel give the most support to the Romans 1:20 – Genesis 1:1 *authorized analogy* of explaining the Trinity (what God's divine nature is like). The key verse scriptures are highlighted in BOLD *ITALICS* and are <u>UNDERLINED</u> at the numbered headings. The other 30 verses give great support to the analogy, but don't have quite the impact as the key verses..

If you have any suggestions, new insights, questions, comments, or corrections, please e-mail me at Godisatrinity1@live.com.

Let's start … at the beginning.

1. Genesis 1:1

1 In the ***beginning*** God created the ***heavens*** and the ***earth***.

This is the key verse, along with Romans 1:20 in explaining the Trinity (what God's divine nature is like).

Time, space, and matter all had their ***beginning*** at the awesome moment of Genesis 1:1. 2 Timothy 1:9 speaks of a grace given to us "before the beginning of time." Hebrews 11:3 speaks of the fact that the visible universe (matter) was not made out of some other seeable matter. It "came" into existence in Genesis 1:1.

Genesis 1:1 very clearly shows us what God's divine nature is like (it makes it seeable and understandable) when you consider that the creation is 100 percent time (time is everywhere), 100 percent space (space is everywhere), and 100 percent matter *simultaneously.* It is 100 percent of each of the three all at once! This *perfectly* demonstrates what God's divine nature is like. He is 100 percent Father, 100 percent Son, and 100 percent Holy Spirit *simultaneously.*

I find it ironic, yet not surprising, that theologians, Bible scholars, and millions upon millions of Jews and Christians alike have searched the scriptures for the last two millennia to learn more about the essence of God's nature and what they were seeking was jumping out at them when they read the very first verse of the Bible. Indeed, God must have a sense of humor.

See Colossians 2:2-3.

*

2. Genesis 1:26

26 Then **God said**, ""Let **us** make man in **our** image, in **our** likeness**, and let them rule over the fish of the sea and the birds of the air, over the livestock, over all the earth, and over all the creatures that move along the ground."

Notice that in this verse God is speaking to Himself, and He says, "Let **US** make man in **OUR** image, in **OUR** likeness. Not only are US, and OUR plural pronouns, they are also repeated three times. Remember, this does not imply that there are three Gods, for the Father, Son, and Holy Spirit are *completely* inseparable, just like you can't separate space, matter, and time.
See also Genesis 3:22 and 11:7.
*

3. Genesis 2:4

4 This is the account of the **heavens** and the **earth when** they were created.

Genesis is divided into nine main sections, each ending with the phrase "This is the account of." For example, it is thought that Adam wrote Genesis 2:4b to Genesis 5:1a and his written record ends in Genesis 5:1a with the words "This is the written account of Adam's line," that phrase being the final "signature" on Adam's account (this made Adam an eye witness of the events about which he wrote). Genesis 5:1b to Genesis 6:9a is the writing of Noah.
The nine main subdivisions of Genesis and their authors are the following:

1. Genesis 1:1 – 2:4 (God)
2. Genesis 2:4b – 5:1 (Adam)
3. Genesis 5:1b – 6:9 (Noah)
4. Genesis 6:9b – 10:1 (sons of Noah)
5. Genesis 10:1b – 11:10 (Shem)
6. Genesis 11:10b – 11:27 (Terah)

7. Genesis 11:27b – 25:19 (Isaac)
8. Genesis 25:19b – 37:2 (Jacob)
9. Genesis 37:2b - Exodus 1:1 (sons of Jacob)

Note that if this theory is correct, God either penned Genesis 1:1 – 2:4 Himself or He sat Adam down and told him the story. God would have had to sit Adam down and tell him the story about Genesis 2:4b-7 also. This does not seem unreasonable or irrational at all. God and Adam apparently had a "perfect" relationship at the time, and I am sure God very much enjoyed telling Adam this information.

An excellent discussion of this literary theory (or hypothesis) can be found in *The Genesis Record* by the late Dr. Henry Morris.

If this hypothesis is correct, Genesis 1:1 to Genesis 2:4a was written by God himself and His "signature" (Genesis 2:4) was "HEAVENS and EARTH WHEN they were created," speaking of space (heavens), matter (earth), and time (when). This does *not* imply that space, matter, and time *are* God, but rather, they reflect His divine nature so perfectly He could use them as His "signature."

Although God is indirectly the author of all scripture through the inspiration of the Holy Spirit, as far as I know, the only other time God *directly* authors a portion of scripture is the writing of the Ten Commandments (see Exodus 31:18). It occurs to me that these two passages actually written by God Himself are both occasions where God wanted to be *very* clear and straightforward with His people. When He said "thou shall not steal,", he actually meant that it was wrong to steal what doesn't belong to you, *and* when He said "for in six days God created the heavens and the earth" (see Exodus 20:11) he meant that He created the heavens and the earth in six *days*, just like it is clearly stated in Genesis Chapter One.

If indeed there is a sense in which God considers time, space, and matter His "signature," it would have far reaching implications for the other places in scripture where time, space, and matter occur together. For a list of 24 of these scriptures, see Appendix I on page 79.

See also Deuteronomy 30:19 where time, space, and matter are called upon by God to "witness" the covenant Moses was making with the Israelites.

*

4. Genesis 11:5-9

5 But *the LORD* came down to see the city and the tower that the men were building. 6 *The LORD* said, "If as one people speaking the same language they have begun to do this, then nothing they plan to do will be impossible for them. 7 Come, let **US** go down and confuse their language so they will not understand each other." 8 So the LORD scattered them from there over all the earth, and they stopped building the city. 9 That is why it was called Babel — because there the LORD confused the language of the whole world. From there the LORD scattered them over the face of the whole earth.

In this passage, when the Lord starts speaking (v. 6), who do you suppose He is speaking to? Who was the "**US**" in this passage? The answer is, the Father was speaking to the Son and the Spirit, or the Son was speaking to the Father and the Spirit, or the Spirit was speaking to the Father and the Son. Notice that in verse 8 it says, "So the LORD (singular) scattered them".

Notice also, in verses 8 and 9 the phrase "the Lord" occurs three times. This is interesting.

*

5. Genesis 13:14-15

14 The LORD said to Abram after Lot had parted from him, "Lift up your eyes from where you are and look **NORTH** and **SOUTH**, **EAST** and **WEST**. 15 All *the land* that you see I will give to you and your offspring *forever*.

The covenant the Lord made with Abram was that He was giving Abram *this much* **SPACE**" (lift up your eyes from where you are and look <u>north</u> and <u>south</u>, <u>east</u> and <u>west</u>), ***this much MATTER*** (the land) and the covenant was to be for ***this much time*** (***forever***).

In Jeremiah 33:19-21 God made a covenant with time, and in Genesis 9:13 God makes a covenant with the earth. In Genesis 13:14-15 the emphasis seems to be on space (north, south, east, and west).

My conclusion is that in making this covenant, the Lord was, in a very real sense giving of Himself. '. In light of the truth of Romans 1:20, it was as if God was inviting His people to *remember who He is* in the blessing He was giving them.

See also Genesis 15:18-21.

*

6. Genesis 35:7

7 There he built an altar, and he called the place El Bethel, because it was there that <u>God</u> revealed himself to him when he was fleeing from his brother.

The word God in this verse is in the ***plural*** in the Hebrew. The only sensible explanation for this is that although there is but one God, He has a "plural" nature unified to such an extent that He is ONE. Time, space, and matter are *completely* unified. That's why they call the creation the UNI-verse.

*

7. Exodus 3:12-16

12 And God said, "<u>I will be with you</u>. And this will be the sign to you that it is I who have sent you: When you have brought the people out of Egypt, you will worship God on this mountain."
13 Moses said to God, "Suppose I go to the Israelites and say to them, 'The God of your fathers has sent me to you,' and they ask me, 'What is his name?' Then what shall I tell them?"

14 God said to Moses, "*__I AM WHO I AM__*. This is what you are to say to the Israelites: 'I AM has sent me to you.'"
15 God also said to Moses, "Say to the Israelites, 'The LORD, the God of your fathers — the God of Abraham, the God of Isaac and the God of Jacob — has sent me to you.' This is my name forever, the name by which I am to be remembered from generation to generation.
16 "Go, assemble the elders of Israel and say to them, 'The LORD, the God of your fathers — the God of Abraham, Isaac and Jacob — *__appeared to me__* and said: I have watched over you and have seen what has been done to you in Egypt.

God is the great I AM, the <u>omnipresent</u> and <u>ever present</u> God. "I AM" is known as the *present tense* in the English language. God is the *great I am*, the God that <u>"is"</u>. He is a reality that we cannot <u>"shake</u> or <u>escape</u> from" or <u>change</u>, no matter how hard we try. He is just <u>"there"</u>.
Now notice all the underlined words in the last paragraph. They all describe God, and they also describe time, space, and matter.

1. Time is omnipresent, ever present, present tense, time "is", we cannot "shake or escape time, and we cannot change time. Time is just "there".
2. Space is omnipresent, ever present, present tense, it "is", we cannot "escape" space, and we cannot change space. Space is just "there".
3. Matter is omnipresent (when matter is considered to be solids, liquids, gases, energy, and light), matter is "ever present, matter is always in the present, we cannot shake or escape from matter, and we cannot destroy matter. Matter is just "there".

*

8. Exodus 25:8-9

8 "Then have them make a sanctuary for me, and I will dwell among them. 9 Make this tabernacle and all its furnishings *exactly like the pattern* I will show you.

Lev 24:7-8
8 This **bread** is to be set out before the LORD **regularly, Sabbath after Sabbath**, on behalf of the Israelites, as a **lasting covenant**.

When I repeat something over, and over, and over again to my child it invariably means *"This is very important to me!"* Exodus 25:9 was instruction from the Lord to construct the tabernacle and *all* its furnishings exactly *like the pattern* God was going to show Moses. These same directions are repeated in Exodus 25:40; 26:30; 27:8; 31:11; 39:32; 39:42; Numbers 8:4; 1 Chronicles 28:11; 28:19; Acts 7:44; and Hebrews 8:5. Something mentioned this much in scripture *must* have been extremely important to God. As a matter of fact, in Exodus 39:43 Moses himself checked all the work the Israelites had done to *make sure* it had been done the way the Lord had shown him on the mountain.

Although I don't feel qualified to comment a lot about the tabernacle, I would like to point something out that is very relevant to our topic (God's divine nature being *perfectly* reflected by time, space, and matter), and that is that God went to great measures to show Moses exactly what **materials (matter)** He wanted him to use in making the tabernacle. God was VERY specific. He wanted it done HIS WAY. God was also VERY SPECIFIC about all the **measurements (how much space)** of the tabernacle. He was VERY SPECIFIC. He wanted it done HIS WAY.

The Lord also gave very specific directions on the length of time He wanted the bread to be set out before Him in His sanctuary (continuously, as a lasting covenant).

So the Lord gave VERY SPECIFIC matter, space, and time instructions in building His tabernacle. How interesting!
*

9. Numbers 6:22-27

22 The LORD said to Moses, 23 "Tell Aaron and his sons, 'This is how you are to bless the Israelites. Say to them:
24 "**The LORD** bless you
and keep you;
25 the **LORD** make his face shine upon you and be gracious to you;
26 the **LORD** turn his face toward you and give you peace.'"
27 "So they will put **my name** on the Israelites, and I will bless them."

It is hard not to "see" the Trinity in this verse. "The Lord" is repeated three times and God Himself says, "This is MY NAME." Also see Isaiah 6:3 and Exodus 34:6.
*

10. Deuteronomy 4:32-36

32 Ask now about the **former days**, long **before your time**, from the day God created man on the **earth**; ask from one end of the **heavens** to the other. Has anything so great as this ever happened, or has anything like it ever been heard of? 33 Has any other people heard the voice of God speaking out of fire, as you have, and lived? 34 Has any god ever tried to take for himself one nation out of another nation, by testings, by miraculous signs and wonders, by war, by a mighty hand and an outstretched arm, or by great and awesome deeds, like all the things the LORD your God did for you in Egypt before your very eyes?
35 You were shown these things so that you might know that the LORD is God; besides him there is no other. 36 From heaven he made you hear his voice to discipline you. On earth he showed you his great fire, and you heard his words from out of the fire.

This is known as "The Lord Is God" passage. Notice time (former days equals past time), earth (matter), and space (heavens) in v. 32. Notice heaven (space), earth, and "heard His words" (this happened over time) in v. 36. Isn't it interesting that the themes of space, matter, and time are present in "The Lord Is God" passage, a passage of scripture that is telling us something about WHO God is?

It seems to be the rule in scripture rather than the exception that when the writer is trying to tell us something about WHO God is, that the theme of time, space, and matter also occurs in the same context.
*

11. Deuteronomy 6:4

4 Hear, O Israel: The LORD our God, the LORD is <u>ONE.</u>

The FACT that there is only ONE God is repeated over and over again in the scriptures. Here is a partial list:

1 Kings 8:60	Nehemiah 9:6	Isaiah 42:8
Mark 12:29 (Jesus speaking)	John 17:3 (Jesus speaking)	1 Corinthians 8:4-6
Galatians 3:20	1 Timothy 2:5	James 2:19

I want to be VERY clear about something. The Christian doctrine of the Trinity and the scriptures themselves has ALWAYS maintained that there is ONLY ONE God. But it is also true that the scriptures describe three distinct "personalities" emanating from the "oneness" of God. If those three distinct personalities could be SEPARATED, then the oneness of the God of the Bible would cease to exist. This fact is what makes the time/space/matter analogy authorized by God himself in Romans 1:20 so awesome. God's own authorized analogy for His divine nature reveals to us that the three "personalities" are

indeed NOT separable, any more than time, space, and matter are separable. God, indeed, is a perfect Trinity.
*

12. Deuteronomy 30:19-20

19 **This day** I call **heaven** and **earth** as **witnesses** against you that I have set before you life and death, blessings and curses. Now choose life, so that you and your children may live 20 and that you may love the LORD your God, listen to his voice, and hold fast to him. For the LORD is your life, and he will give you many years in the land he swore to give to your fathers, Abraham, Isaac and Jacob.

When I first "saw" this passage of scripture my spirit felt over-whelmed. "This day (very specific point in time) I call heaven (space) and earth (matter) as WITNESSES AGAINST YOU that I have set before you life and death, blessings and curses." The notes on Deut. 30:19 in the NIV Study Bible make the following statement:
"The typical ancient covenant outside the Old Testament contained a list of gods who served as "witnesses" to its provisions (the Suzerain-Vassal Treaty is an example. To read about this treaty, go to: http://webmail.mobap.edu/schulten/LegalModels.OTCovenants1. htm) The Covenant in Deuteronomy was "witnessed" by heaven and earth." I would emphasize also that Moses very emphatically set the witness of heaven and earth within a very specific time frame, "this day". I find it astounding that Moses, in trying to follow the tradition of his time was inspired to call HEAVEN (space) and EARTH (matter) as witnesses within a very specific TIME frame (this day). As was the tradition of the Jews, Moses knew he couldn't use the name of God Himself (Elohim), so Moses, in a sense on the spot, said "this day, I call heaven and earth as witnesses." It would really be interesting to find out if Moses actually knew the significance of what he was saying, or whether he was just being "sensitive to the Spirit of God" when he said that. It was, however, VERY apparent that Moses didn't believe that heaven and earth were actually gods.

I believe with all my heart that Moses wrote what he did in Deut. 30:19 because there was NO ONE EXCEPT GOD HIMSELF that was worthy of being a witness to this covenant, and time, space, and matter so closely reflects God's divine nature that they were the "next best thing". It bears repeating here, that neither Moses nor I am saying that space, matter, and time *is* God, but rather, God's divine nature can Be *clearly seen*, and *understood* by beholding space, matter, and time, and as such they are worthy of being mentioned on this solemn occasion.

See also Deut. 4:25-26; 31:28; 32:1; Psalms 50:1-7 and notes in the NIV Study Bible for Psalms 50:1; Isaiah 1:2.

If I have a reader who is saying to himself / herself, "heaven and earth were witnesses, but NOT TIME, which, in your analogy of space, matter and time being analogous to Father, Son, and Holy Spirit leaves out the Holy Spirit", I would point out the following:

1. Just like time is the "ever present background" of all things that happen to matter in space, time WAS the ever present background during this solemn occasion.
2. The Holy Spirit "testifies" or "witnesses" in other places in scripture. In Nehemiah 9:30 the scripture says "For many years you were patient with them. By your Spirit you **admonished** them through your prophets. Yet they paid no attention, so you handed them over to the neighboring peoples.

The word ADMONISHED in that verse is the same Hebrew word as is used in Deuteronomy 30:19 for "witnesses". The Holy Spirit witnessed to the people through the prophets.
*

13. Joshua 3:10

10 This is how you will <u>know</u> that **the living God** is among you and that he will certainly drive out before you the Canaanites, Hittites, Hivites, Perizzites, Girgashites, Amorites and Jebusites.

In this verse of scripture God is called "the LIVING God". One important characteristic of all living things (this may not be true for some "lower forms" of life, but it is certainly true of the "higher forms") is that they are mobile. They can *move*.

Living things (composed of matter) are *experience-able* over time as they move in space. Notice that if time, space or matter were to cease to exist, God could not be experienced (because all of reality would cease to exist).

*

14. 2 Samuel 7:22

22 "How great you are, O Sovereign LORD! **There is no one like you**, and **there is no God but you**, as we have heard with our own ears".

King David says, "There is no ONE like you (no person or thing), and there is NO GOD but you". All the other "false gods" are not gods at all. They are merely false (untrue, or a god that doesn't actually exist). When David said, "There is no one LIKE you", he was essentially saying there is no ONE, no person or being worthy of being compared to God. Isaiah 40:18 says, "To *whom* then, will you compare God?" The obvious implication from the scripture is: *nobody*! God does not allow Himself to be compared to anything. However, He DOES allow Himself to be *contrasted* with time, space, and matter (see #18, Psalms 102:25-27).

*

15. 1 Kings 8:23

"O LORD, God of Israel, there is no God like you in heaven above or on earth below-you who keep your covenant of love with your servants who continue wholeheartedly in your way.

This passage stresses the "singleness and oneness" of God (there is no God like you) with time (there is) space (in heaven) and matter (on earth) in the same context.

See also Deuteronomy 4:32-36.

*

16. 2 Kings 19:15-16

15 And Hezekiah prayed to the LORD: "O LORD, God of Israel, enthroned between the cherubim, ***you alone are God*** over all the kingdoms of the earth. You ***have made heaven*** and ***earth***. 16 Give ear, O LORD, and hear; open your eyes, O LORD, and see; listen to the words Sennacherib has sent to insult the ***living God***.

In Hezekiah's prayer to God it is as if he is reminding God "who He is". This passage encapsulates the character and nature of God perfectly. It speaks of God's exclusiveness (you alone are God), God's divine nature (time, space, and matter), and that God is EXPERIENCABLE (living God).

During the days of the writing of the Old and New Testament of the Bible, pagan gods that didn't exist, were plentiful (see Jeremiah 10:11-12). So when the writers of scripture needed to make *very* clear which God they were referring to, it became necessary to "qualify" or "describe" the God of the Bible. So God was called "God, Creator / Maker of heaven and earth" eighteen times in the Old Testament, and two times in the New. He is also called "God of heaven and earth" six times in the Old Testament, and three times in the New. Those phrases were used to make sure everyone knew EXACTLY who the writer was talking about.

Consider these verses: Genesis 14:19; 14:22, 2 Kings 19:15, 1 Chronicles 16:26, 2 Chronicles 2:12, Nehemiah 9:5-6, Psalm 115:15; 121:2; 124:8; 134:3; 146:5-6, Isaiah 37:16-17; 51:13, Jeremiah 10:12; 32:17; 51:15, Acts 4:24; 14:15

*

17. Job 11:7-9

7 "Can you fathom the mysteries of God?
Can you probe the limits of the Almighty?
8 They are **_higher_** than the heavens-what can you do?
They are **_deeper_** than the depths of the grave-what can you
know?
9 Their measure is **_longer_** than the earth
and **_wider_** than the sea.

The mysteries of God are here described as an area of **space**. See
#50 Ephesians 3:17-19.

The sum total of what we can KNOW about God is the sum total
of EXACTLY what God wishes to reveal about Himself. In Romans
1:19-20, in conjunction with Genesis 1:1, we can KNOW that God
wishes to reveal what his divine nature is like, and it is revealed as
a PERFECT TRINITY.
*

18. Psalm 102:25-27

25 In the **_BEGINNING_** you laid the foundations of the
EARTH,
and the **_HEAVENS_** are the work of your hands.
26 **THEY** will perish, **BUT YOU** remain;
they will all wear out like a garment.
Like clothing you will change them
and **_they_** will be discarded.
27 **_But you_** remain the same, and your years will never end.

In this passage, **time** (the beginning), **matter** (earth), and **space**
(heavens) are **_CONTRASTED_** with **God Himself**. To contrast
means to "compare in order to show unlikeness or differences". The
differences noted are that time, space, and matter will parish, but
God will remain (forever).

I have searched the scriptures, and have found NOTHING
except time, space, and matter that God considers worthy of being

CONTRASTED with Him. At first glance, the reader of Jeremiah 10:11-16 my think that God is contrasting Himself with false gods "who did not make the heavens and the earth", but after a careful reading you will see that in verse 16 it is said that God "is not like these". They are complete opposites.

Psalms 102:25-27 has a parallel passage in Hebrews 1:8-12 in which time, space, and matter are CONTRASTED with the **Son Jesus**, which, of course, is not a problem since he is God, and "in Christ, all the fullness of the Deity lives in bodily form." (See Colossians 2:9.)

It is also important to point out, that since Psalms 102:25-27 and Hebrews 1:10-12 are actually talking about the Son (Jesus), than the Son is ETERNAL, and His years will NEVER end. The Son was indeed, God in the flesh.

Also, Mark 13:31 makes it clear that the creation (time, space, and matter) cannot be, and never has been God (as a Pantheist would affirm), because they will "pass away", but God will NEVER pass away.

See also Luke 21:33; Isaiah 51:5-6.
*

19. Psalm 103:12

12 As far as the *east* is from the *west*, so far has he removed our transgressions from us.

Notice that because of what Jesus did on the cross, God has put **SPACE** between us and our sins. Applying the analogy authorized by Romans 1:20, the Father has put Himself (along with His Son, Jesus, and the Holy Spirit, who cannot be separated form the Father) between us and our sins. Thank you Lord.
*

20. Psalm 125:2

2 As the mountains surround Jerusalem,
so ***the LORD surrounds his people***
both now and forevermore.

Notice please, that there are only 4 (four) "things" that <u>surround</u> God's people (believers). They are:

1. God - God COMPLETELY surrounds His people. He's in every nook and cranny.
2. Time - Time COMPLETELY surrounds us. There is no place where time doesn't exist.
3. Space- Space COMPLETELY surrounds us. There is no place where space doesn't exist.
4. Matter- Matter COMPLETELY surrounds us. There is No place where matter doesn't exist.

Again, it bears repeating here that time, space, and matter are NOT God, (see Psalms 102:25-27) they just reflect His divine nature so PERFECTLY that we can "clearly see" and "understand" the essence of his divine nature by understanding time, space, and matter. Time, space, and matter are no more God than the clay pot is the potter.
*

21. Psalm 139:7-10

7 Where can I go from your ***Spirit?***
Where can I flee from *your presence*?
8 If I go up to the ***heavens***, you are there;
if I make my bed in the depths (of the ***earth***), you are there.
9 If I rise on the wings of the dawn,
if I settle on the far side of the sea,
10 even there your hand will guide me,
your right hand will hold me fast.

This passage speaks of the OMNIPRESENSE of the Holy Spirit. Notice that when God seeks to establish the omnipresence of the Holy Spirit in scripture, the HEAVENS (space) and the earth (matter) are in the same context. This is because time, space, and matter can NOT be separated, just like the Father, Son, and Holy Spirit can not be separated.
*

22. Psalm 148:1-14

1 Praise the LORD.
Praise the LORD from the **heavens**, praise him in the heights above. 2 Praise him, all his angels, praise him, all his heavenly hosts. 3 Praise him, **sun** and **moon**, praise him, all you shining **stars.** 4 Praise him, you **highest heavens** and you waters above the skies. 5 Let them praise the name of the LORD, for he commanded and they were created. 6 He set them in place **for ever and ever**; he gave a decree that will never pass away.
7 Praise the LORD from the **earth**, you great sea creatures and all ocean depths, 8 lightning and hail, snow and clouds, stormy winds that do his bidding, 9 you **mountains** and all hills, fruit trees and all cedars, 10 **wild animals** and all cattle, small creatures and flying birds, 11 kings of the earth and all nations, you princes and all rulers on earth, 12 young men and maidens, old men and children.
13 Let them praise the name of the LORD, for his name alone is exalted; his splendor IS above the EARTH and the HEAVENS. 14 He has raised up for his people a horn, the praise of all his saints, of Israel, the people close to his heart. Praise the LORD.

In this passage, all of creation (time, space, and matter) is praising God. The creation is subject to God, just as the clay pot is subject to the potter.

See also Psalms 8:1; 57:5; 57:11; 99:2-3; 108:5; 113:4; Isaiah 44:23.

*

23. Isaiah 40:18-28

Besides Genesis 1:1 and Deuteronomy 30:19, this passage is perhaps the best Old Testament confirmation that God authorizes the time/space/matter analogy to reveal His divine nature. Below is a comparison of Isaiah 40:18-28 with Romans 1:20 and Genesis 1:1. The comparison is astounding.

Romans 1:20

1

For **since the creation of the world**

God's invisible qualities,

2

His eternal power and **divine nature**

3

have been **clearly seen** ,

4

being **understood**

5

from what has been **made** ,

6

so that they are **without excuse**.

Genesis 1:1

7

In the **beginning**

8

God **created**

9

the **heavens**

10

and the **earth**.

Isaiah 40:18-28

18 To whom then, will you compare God?
What image will you compare him to?

19 As for an idol, a craftsman casts it,

a goldsmith overlays it with gold and

fashions silver chains for it. 20 A man

too poor to present such an offering

selects wood that will not rot. He

looks for a skilled craftsman to set up

an idol that will not topple.

4

21 Do you not **know**? Have you not

heard? Has it not been told you from

1,7

the **beginning**?

(Romans 1:20 and Genesis 1:1   /   Isaiah 40:18-28 comparison continued)

1
For **since the creation of the world**

God's invisible qualities,
2
His eternal power and **divine nature**
3
have been **clearly seen** ,
4
being **understood**
5
from what has been **made** ,
6
so that they are **without excuse**.

Genesis 1:1
7
In the **beginning**
8
God **created**
9
the **heavens**
10
and the **earth**.

4
Have you not **understood** since the
10   1,8
earth was **founded**?

22 He sits enthroned above the circle of
5,10
the **earth**, and its people are like

grasshoppers . He stretches out the
9
heavens like a canopy, and spreads

them out like a tent to live in. ....

v25 **"To whom will you compare me?**

Or who is my equal?", says the Holy

One. 26 Lift up your eyes and look to
5,9   5,8
the **heavens**: Who **created** all these?
4
v28 Do you not **know**? Have you not

heard? The Lord is the everlasting God
8   5,10
the **creator** of the ends of the **earth**.

Indeed, Isaiah 40:18-28 may have been the Apostle Paul's inspiration and confirmation from the Holy Spirit (remember, the Holy Spirit makes it possible to EXPERIENCE God) when he wrote Romans 1:20. Some things, such as the divine nature of God, never change; indeed they CANNOT CHANGE, and obviously the Apostle Paul knew that.
*

24. Isaiah 48:12-13

12 "Listen to me, O Jacob,
Israel, whom I have called:
I am he; **I am** the **first** and **I am** the **last**.

13 My own hand laid the foundations of the **earth**,
and my right hand spread out the **heavens**;
when I summon them,
they all stand up together.

In this verse, God is identifying himself. He says, "I am he." And then God says, "I am (the PRESENT TENSE of time) the first (the PAST TENSE of time) and I am the last (the FUTURE TENSE of time)." Then He identifies Himself as the God who created the **earth** and the **heavens**. He is THAT God, the ONLY God. Notice that God's identity is intricately woven in time, space, and matter, for what He is like (what His divine nature is like) can be UNDERSTOOD by examining time, space, and matter (see Romans 1:20 and chapter 1 of this book).
*

25. Jeremiah 23:24

24 Can anyone hide in secret places
so that I cannot see him?"
declares the LORD.
"Do not **I fill heaven and earth?"**
declares the LORD.

Notice that there are only four "things" that FILL heaven and earth. They are:

1. **God** (Father, Son, and Holy Spirit)
2. **Time** (analogous to the Holy Spirit in the analogy authorized by Romans 1:20)
3. **Space** (analogous to the Father in the analogy authorized by Romans 1:20)
4. **Matter** (analogous to the Son in the analogy authorized by Romans 1:20)

This makes it very easy to see that God's divine nature is PERFECTLY reflected by what He made in Genesis 1:1 (time, space, and matter).

*

26. Jeremiah 33:23-26

23 The word of the LORD came to Jeremiah: 24 "Have you not noticed that these people are saying, 'The LORD has rejected the two kingdoms he chose'? So they despise my people and no longer regard them as a nation. 25 This is what the LORD says: 'If I have not established my **covenant** with **day** and **night AND** the **fixed laws** of **heaven** and **earth**, 26 then I will reject the descendants of Jacob and David my servant and will not choose one of his sons to rule over the descendants of Abraham, Isaac, and Jacob. For I will restore their fortunes and have compassion on them.'"

Is it possible that God had made a covenant with time, space, and matter? That is exactly what Jeremiah 33:25 says! (Note also that Jeremiah 33:20 speaks of God's covenant with time, and in Genesis 9:13 God makes a covenant with earth, i.e. matter).

The fixed laws of heaven (space) and earth (matter) refers to the fixed physical laws that God put in place that **govern how space and matter interact over time**. For a complete list of these laws, go to this Web site:

http://en.wikipedia.org/wiki/List_of_laws_in_science

ALL of the physical laws God put in place CANNOT and WILL NOT violate the fact that God's divine nature is PERFECTLY reflected in the time, space, matter continuum that God created in Genesis 1:1.

The fact that God made a COVENANT with time, space, and matter blows my mind. It doesn't surprise me, but it blows my mind.

See also Jeremiah 33:19-21 (God makes a covenant with time), and Genesis 9:13 (God makes a covenant with the earth). See also Deuteronomy 30:19.
*

27. Matthew 17:1-9

Matt 17:1-9

17:1 After six days Jesus took with him Peter, James and John the brother of James, and led them up a high mountain by themselves. 2 There he was TRANSFIGURED before them. His face shone like the *sun*, and his clothes became as *white as the light*. 3 Just then there appeared before them Moses and Elijah, talking with Jesus.
4 Peter said to Jesus, "Lord, it is good for us to be here. If you wish, I will put up three shelters-one for you, one for Moses, and one for Elijah."
5 While he was still speaking, a bright cloud enveloped them, and a voice from the cloud said, "This is my Son, whom I love; with him I am well pleased. Listen to him!"
6 When the disciples heard this, they fell facedown to the ground, terrified. 7 But Jesus came and touched them. "Get up," he said. "Don't be afraid." 8 When they looked up, they saw no one except Jesus.
9 As they were coming down the mountain, Jesus instructed them, "Don't tell anyone what you have seen, until the Son of Man has been raised from the dead."

Most Bibles call this passage of scripture "The Mount of Transfiguration.". Actually, the real transfiguration took place in a stable in Bethlehem 33 years earlier. Peter, James, and John saw Jesus, the son of God in his *natural state*. Hebrews 1:3 says "**The Son is** the *radiance* of **God's** glory and *the exact representation of his being.* Peter, James, and John SAW the radiance of God's glory on that day. 1 John 1:5 says "God is light, and in him there is no darkness at all." Peter, James, and John saw the "fullness" of God, that is, Jesus in his glorified body.

*

28. Matthew 27:45-54

45 From the sixth hour until the ninth hour darkness (of the skies, i.e. space) came over all the land. 46 About the ninth hour Jesus cried out in a loud voice, "Eloi, Eloi, lama sabachthani?"- which means, "My God, my God, why have you forsaken me?"

47 When some of those standing there heard this, they said, "He's calling Elijah."

48 Immediately one of them ran and got a sponge. He filled it with wine vinegar, put it on a stick, and offered it to Jesus to drink. 49 The rest said, "Now leave him alone. Let's see if Elijah comes to save him." 50 And when Jesus had cried out again in a loud voice, he gave up his Spirit.

51 **At that moment** the curtain of the temple was torn in two from top to bottom. The **earth shook** and the **rocks split**. 52 The tombs broke open and the bodies of many holy people who had died were raised to life. 53 They came out of the tombs, and after Jesus' resurrection they went into the holy city and appeared to many people.

54 When the centurion and those with him who were guarding Jesus saw the **earthquake** and all that had happened, they were terrified, and exclaimed, **"Surely he was the Son of God!"**

Many of the verses in this Bible study are very thought provoking, but this one may be my favorite. 2 Corinthians 5:21 says the following: 21 "God made him who had no sin **to be sin** for us, so that in him we might become the righteousness of God". When Jesus screamed out "My God, my God, why have you forsaken me?" Jesus was experiencing the agony of SEPARATION FROM THE FATHER <u>for the first time in eternity</u>. The scripture says that God's eyes are too pure to look upon evil, He cannot "fellowship" with sin. (See Habakkuk 1:13) That separation from the Father was so agonizing that Jesus screamed out in agony.

So what was happening "*in the SPIRIT*" was a separation between the Father and the Son for the first time in history. Those standing there watching the crucifixion had no clue as to what was happening, or its awesome significance for mankind. How such a "separation" could have happened is not at all apparent. For in our physical world, space CANNOT separate from matter.

But notice, while the separation between the Father and the Son was taking place, what was happening *in the NATURAL*? Verse 51: At THAT MOMENT (time) the SKIES (space) got dark, the curtain of the temple was torn in two, the EARTH (matter) shook, the ROCKS split. Could it be, and this is ONLY speculation, that just as the Father and the Son had a "separation" because of sin, that NATURE WAS GOING NUTS? Could it be that space and matter were trying to "separate", and were RESPONDING to what was happening in the Spirit to its creator? The creation's reaction to what was happening (skies dark, rocks splitting, earth shaking) were all given as a "sign" for those watching, but this would actually explain *why* it happened (not HOW it happened, but why it happened). I hope this does not seem too far fetched. But after you get the UNDERSTANDING of the Trinity in your spirit as I have, this kind of speculation flows naturally from your spirit. To me, what you have just read is MIND BOGGLING.
*

29. Matthew 28:19-20

19 Therefore go and make disciples of all nations, baptizing them **in the name** of the **Father** and of the **Son** and of the **Holy Spirit**,

This is an obvious "Trinity verse", but now you know that Matthew was referring to the ONE and ONLY GOD of scripture who is capable of manifesting Himself in three distinct ways. Why would Jesus tell his disciples to baptize in the name of the Father and of the Son and of the Holy Spirit if they were not all God?
*

30. Luke 10:17-21

17 The seventy-two returned with *joy* and said, "Lord, even **the demons submit** to us in your name."
18 He replied, "I saw Satan fall like lightning from heaven.
19 I have given you authority to trample on snakes and scorpions and to overcome all the power of the enemy; nothing will harm you. 20 However, do not **rejoice** that the spirits submit to you, but **rejoice** that your names are written in heaven."
21 **At that time Jesus**, full of **joy** through the **Holy Spirit**, said, "I praise you, **Father**, Lord of **heaven** and **earth**, because you have hidden these things from the wise and learned, and revealed them to little children. Yes, Father, for this was your good pleasure.

Just like Exodus 3:14 is the CLEAREST expression of God's NAME in the scriptures, Luke 10:21 is the CLEAREST expression of what God's divine nature is like in the entire Bible.

In this verse of scripture the Father, Son, and Holy Spirit are all REJOICING TOGETHER, and TIME, SPACE, and MATTER are all three mentioned in the same context.

I would like to suggest that in Verse 21, the phrase "At that time" has no other function than to have TIME, space, and matter all mentioned in this context. In other words, the Holy Spirit inspired the writing of "At that time" just to help us clearly see and understand what God's divine nature is like.

I can see God's divine nature "bubbling over" or "flowing out of" this text. The New King James Spirit Filled Life Bible notes on Luke 10:21 say the following:

"The successful mission of the 70 disciples caused Jesus to burst forth in a spontaneous demonstration of worship IN THE SPIRIT (the Greek word suggests shouting and leaping with joy)." God is having His own personal worship time, and His divine nature is written all over it.

Do you want to make God joyful and encourage Him to "show up" in His fullness Then be born again (John 3), be filled with the Holy Spirit (Acts 2), and cast out demons in his name (Luke 10:17).

Whether or not these New Testament word associations have any theological or doctrinal significance I do not know. However, I find it fascinating that in the New Testament alone the following word associations occur in the same context:

Holy Spirit / Son / Father: 25 times
Time / Son/ Father: 20 times
Time/ Matter / Space: 4 times
Spirit / Son / Space: 4 times
Time / Son / Space: 3 times
Spirit / Matter / Space: 1 time

See Appendix II on page 87 for these references.

*

31. Luke 12:12

12 for the **Holy Spirit** will teach you <u>at that time</u> what you should say."

Note that the Holy Spirit and time are used in the same context. The same is true in Isaiah 59:21 "As for me, this is my covenant with them," says the LORD. "My Spirit, who is on you, and my words that I have put in your mouth will not depart from your mouths, or from the mouths of your children, or from the mouths of their descendants <u>from this time on and forever</u>," says the LORD.
*

32. Luke 24:30-31

30 When he was at the table with them, he took bread, gave thanks, broke it and began to give it to them. 31 Then their eyes were opened and they recognized him, and he **disappeared** from their sight.

Notice that after the resurrection Jesus could be visible or invisible at will. In the Trinity analogy authorized by Romans 1:20 Jesus is analogous to matter, and there are VISIBLE (the seeable elements and light) and INVISIBLE (most gases) forms of MATTER.
*

33. Luke 24:36-39

36 While they were still talking about this, Jesus himself stood among them and said to them, "Peace be with you."
37 They were startled and frightened, thinking they saw a ghost. 38 He said to them, "Why are you troubled, and why do doubts rise in your minds? 39 Look at my **hands** and my **feet**. It is I myself! **Touch me** and see; **a ghost does not have flesh and bones, as you see I have.**"

One of the foundational doctrines of Christianity is the BODILY RESURRECTION of Jesus. After the resurrection Jesus was STILL real matter that could either be visible, or invisible at his will. Of course, this had to be so, or God's divine nature would have been forever CHANGED, and of course, that cannot happen (see Malachi 3:6).
*

34. John 1:1-2

1:1 In the **beginning** was the **Word,** and the Word was with **God,** and the Word was God.
2 He was with **God** in the **beginning.**

In the beginning (time) was the Word (Jesus the Son), and the Word was with God (the Father), and the Word WAS GOD. Notice, dear friends, that Jesus, the Word, was WITH God, and WAS God at the same time (simultaneously). What a wonderful picture of the Trinity.
*

35. John 1:18

18 **No one has ever seen God**, but God the One and Only, who is at the Father's side, has made him known.

No one has EVER SEEN GOD the FATHER, except the Son. God the Father is not seeable on this side of heaven. He may be seeable in heaven, but he is NOT seeable here on earth.

Notice that God the Father is not seeable, just as SPACE is not seeable. Any time you look at something, all you can see is MATTER IN SPACE, but you can NOT see space, just like you cannot see God the Father.

See John 5:37; Matthew 6:6; John 6:46

*

36. John 8:58-59

58 "I tell you the truth," Jesus answered, "before Abraham was born, **I am!**" 59 At this, they picked up stones to stone him, but Jesus hid himself, slipping away from the temple grounds.

What an awesome moment in history this must have been. Jesus, the Son of God, stood among His chosen people and declared Himself to be the great "I AM," the awesome God who spoke to Moses on Mr. Sinai. (See Exodus 3:1-14). It was perfectly proper for Jesus to make this claim, for Jesus and the Father are ONE (see No. 37) and Jesus was just as "present" at the burning bush as the Father (and the Holy Spirit), for Jesus and the Father can no more be separated than space and matter can be separated.

*

37. John 10:30-33, 37-38

30 *"I and the Father are one."*

31 Again the Jews picked up stones to stone him, 32 but Jesus said to them, "I have shown you many great miracles from the Father. For which of these do you stone me?"
33 "We are not stoning you for any of these," replied the Jews, "but for blasphemy, because you, a mere man, *claim to be God*." ....
....

37 Do not believe me unless *I do what my Father does*. 38 But if I do it, even though you do not believe me, believe the miracles, that you may know and understand that *the Father is in me, and I in the Father."* 39 Again they tried to seize him, but he escaped their grasp.

Recalling what you read in Chapter 1 of this book, what was created in Genesis 1:1 was time, space, and matter, and the universe is 100 percent of each of the three simultaneously. The three are completely and totally inseparable. You can't take time out of space and matter; you can't take space out of time and matter; and you can't take matter out of time and space. The three "flow together" PERFECTLY.

Romans 1:20 tells us that God's divine nature can be CLEARLY SEEN and UNDERSTOOD by beholding the "things that were made" in Genesis 1:1. The following verses of scripture speak of the Father, the Son, and the Holy Spirit "existing in the same exact location" SIMULTANEOUSLY:

Matthew 10:40 He who receives me, receives the one who sent me. (Receiving the Father and Son simultaneously.)

John 10:30-39 I and the Father are *one*; and the Father is **in me**, and **I in the Father.)** (They simultaneously occupy the same area of space.)

John 14:9-11 **I am *in the Father*, and the *Father is in me*.** (They both simultaneously occupy the same area of space.)

John 14:16-20 *I am in my Father*, and *you are in me*, and *I am in you*-.

1 Corinthians 3:16 *The Holy Spirit lives in you*. (The Holy Spirit and YOU SIMULTANEOUSLY occupy the same area of space.)

Colossians 1:27 *Christ IN YOU*- (You and Christ occupy the same area of space SIMULTANEOUSLY.)

So the PHYSICAL nature of the God of the Bible is PERFECTLY displayed by time, space, and matter.
*

38. John 15:26-27

26 "When the Counselor comes, whom **I** will send to you **from the Father**, the **Spirit of truth** who **goes out from the Father**, he will **testify about me.**

The Holy Spirit "goes out from" the Father and testifies about Jesus. Is this like saying that TIME "emerges from" SPACE, and TIME testifies (to bear witness; give or afford evidence; affirm as fact or truth) about MATTER? Without TIME, there would be no EVIDENCE, no EXPERIENCE of ANY kind. No "consciousness" of MATTER. To experience matter, you MUST have a continuum of time over which to experience it.
The analogy just keeps getting more perfect.
*

39. John 16:12-14

13 But when he, the Spirit of truth, comes, he will guide you into all truth. **He will not speak on his own; he will speak only what he hears**, and he will tell you what is yet to come.

The Holy Spirit is not a "free agent" that can do his "own thing". The Spirit "goes out from" the Father (see #38). The Holy Spirit cannot be separated from the Father any more than time can be separated from space.

*

40. John 17:2-3

John 17:2-3
2 For you granted him authority over all people that he might give eternal life to all those you have given him. 3 Now this is eternal life: that they may **know you, the only true God, and Jesus Christ, whom you have sent.**

See also Galatians 6:8 (we reap eternal life from the Holy Spirit) and Ephesians 1:17.

Obviously, knowing how to explain the Trinity (knowing how to explain the essence of God's divine nature) is not necessary for obtaining salvation. It has NOTHING to do with whether you are saved or not. That being said, the very definition of eternal life (spending eternity with God) is to KNOW the Lord.

Here is something I find extremely interesting. In both the Old and New Testaments the words "know" and "knew" are used to mean "had marital relations with". Here are several examples:

In the Old Testament, the Hebrew word for knew and know is yada, Strong's lexicon number 3045. All of the following verses of scripture that have the words "knew and know" in them are all the word yada. They are all from the King James Version of the Bible.

Genesis 4:1
4:1 And Adam **knew** Eve his wife; and she conceived, and bare Cain, and said, I have gotten a man from the LORD.
KJV

Genesis 4:17

17 And Cain **knew** his wife; and she conceived, and bare Enoch: and he built a city, and called the name of the city, after the name of his son, Enoch.
KJV

Genesis 4:25
25 And Adam **knew his wife again**; and she bare a son, and called his name Seth: For God, said she, hath appointed me another seed instead of Abel, whom Cain slew.
KJV

Genesis 38:26
26 And Judah acknowledged them, and said, She hath been more righteous than I; because that I gave her not to Shelah my son. And **he knew her again no more**.
KJV

Judges 2:10
10 And also all that generation were gathered unto their fathers: and there arose another generation after them, which **knew not the LORD**, nor yet the works which he had done for Israel.
KJV

Judges 11:39
39 And it came to pass at the end of two months that she returned unto her father, who did with her according to his vow which he had vowed: and **she knew no man**.
KJV

Judges 19:25
25 But the men would not hearken to him: so the man took his concubine, and brought her forth unto them; and **they knew her, and abused her** all the night until the morning: and when the day began to spring, they let her go.
KJV

1 Samuel 1:19-20

19 And they rose up in the morning early, and worshipped before the LORD, and returned, and came to their house to Ramah: and **Elkanah knew Hannah his wife**; and the LORD remembered her. 20 Wherefore it came to pass, when the time was come about after **Hannah had conceived**, that she bare a son, and called his name Samuel, saying, Because I have asked him of the LORD.
KJV

Genesis 18:17-19

17 And the LORD said, Shall I hide from Abraham that thing which I do; 18 Seeing that Abraham shall surely become a great and mighty nation, and all the nations of the earth shall be blessed in him? 19 **For I know him**, that he will command his children and his household after him, and they shall keep the way of the LORD, to do justice and judgment; that the LORD may bring upon Abraham that which he hath spoken of him.
KJV

In the New Testament, the Greek word for knew and know is ginosko, lexicon number 1097. In the following verses from the King James Version, all the words knew and know are all ginosko.

Matthew 1:24-25

24 Then Joseph being raised from sleep did as the angel of the Lord had bidden him, and took unto him his wife: 25 And **knew** her not till she had brought forth her firstborn son: and he called his name JESUS.
KJV

Matthew 7:22-23

22 Many will say to me in that day, Lord, Lord, have we not prophesied in thy name? and in thy name have cast out devils? and in thy name done many wonderful works?

23 And then will I profess unto them, I never **knew** you: depart from me, ye that work iniquity.
KJV

John 17:3
3 And this is life eternal, that they might **KNOW** thee the only true God, and Jesus Christ, whom thou hast sent.
KJV

In all of these verses, the words knew and know imply a great FAMILIARITY (or in the case of Judges 2:10, a great UNFAMILIARITY) among its participants. A married man and woman are privileged to KNOW their partner's PHYSICAL characteristics. If a married man is bruised by a fall, an attentive wife will *know* when he is healed. That is her privilege to *know* her husband's physical characteristics.

In the same way, if you now *know* something about God's *physical* characteristics you could be said to be "privileged". Upon reading and understanding this book, you have that privilege. You now "know" God in a way you didn't before.

See also Ephesians 1:17; 2 Peter 1:2.

*

41. John 17:8

8 For I gave them the words you gave me and they accepted them. They knew with certainty that **I came from you**, and they believed that you sent me.

I am by no means a Greek scholar, and I am more than willing to get input from those of you who are. That being said, the Greek word for "came from" in this verse is exerchomai (#1831 in Strong's Exhaustive Concordance). It means literally to "issue," "come out of," or "depart out of." The dictionary defines "issue" as "the act of sending out or putting forth." I believe that Jesus "coming out of" the Father means much more than "Jesus was in the Father's presence and He came here". The King James Version of the scriptures translates this verse thus:

John 17:8 For I have given unto them the words which thou gavest me; and they have received them, and have known surely that <u>I came out from thee</u>, and they have believed that thou didst send me.
KJV

To "come out of" or "depart out of" the Father is quite different from "to come from the Father". To say a baby "came out of the womb" is different than saying "the man came from Jerusalem." The baby "coming out of" the womb also takes with it the NATURE and DNA of its two parents. Jesus "issued from" the Father, bringing "God's DNA" with him.

Notice also, that in John 15:26 the Holy Spirit "goes out from" the Father.

See also 1 John 5:20.

*

42. Acts 7:54-56

55 But Stephen, **full of the Holy Spirit**, looked **up to heaven** and saw the glory of **God**, and **Jesus** standing at the right hand of **God**. 56 "Look," he said, "I see **heaven** open and the **Son of Man** standing at the right hand of **God**."

Notice how the **Holy Spirit** made it possible for Stephen to **EXPERIENCE** the Father and the Son, just like **TIME** makes it possible to **EXPERIENCE** space and matter. It is not until the Holy Spirit "moves" upon your spirit in the born again experience (see John, Chapter 3) that it is even possible to KNOW the Father and the Son (see John 17:3). Until that happens, all you have is a RELIGION, not a personal relationship with the LIVING and EXPERIENCIBLE GOD.

*

43. Acts 17:27-28

27 God did this so that men would seek him and perhaps reach out for him and find him, though he is not far from each one of us. 28 'For **in him** we <u>live</u> and <u>move</u> and <u>have our being</u>.' As some of your own poets have said, 'We are his offspring.'

Notice that IN GOD we live and move and have our being; and IN SPACE we live and move and have our being, and IN TIME we live and move and have our being, and IN MATTER (completely surrounded by matter) we live and move and have our being.

Verse 28 says "in him (God) we live and move and have our being". John 14:20 says:

"On that day you will realize that **I am in my Father**, and **you are in me**, and **I am in you.**" The statement that we are IN God, of course, has spiritual implications, but it also has a PHYSICAL application. God (the Father AND the Son AND the Holy Spirit) is OMNIPRESENT (everywhere at once). The space that your body now occupies and moves in (in Him we live and move and have our being) is FILLED with God Himself (see Jeremiah 23:24). Your body is also COMPLETELY filled with time, space, and matter. God indeed is not far from each one of us (v. 27).

*

44. Romans 1:19-20

19 since what may be **known about God** is plain to them, because God has made it **plain** to them. 20 For **since the creation of the world** God's invisible qualities-his eternal power and **divine nature**-have been **clearly seen**, being **understood** from **what has been made**, so that men are **without excuse**.

This is the KEY verse (in combination with Genesis 1:1) in the scriptures to understanding what God's divine nature is like, and when you understand what God's divine nature is like, the Trinity opens up like a flower on a spring morning, in all it's radiance and glory. "Seeing" this scripture is truly finding wisdom and knowledge HIDDEN in Christ. (See Colossians 2:1-3).

The specific instructions in Romans 1:20 are to go back in the scriptures to where the world was created (Genesis 1:1) and behold what came into existence there, and that will tell us something about what God's divine nature is like. And when we do see what God's divine nature is like, it should be CLEARLY SEEABLE, and it should be UNDERSTANDABLE, so much so that we are without excuse not to see and understand it. What God created in Genesis 1:1 was time, space, and matter. The creation is 100 percent time, 100 percent space, and 100 percent matter SIMULTANEOUSLY, just like God is 100 percent Father, 100 percent Son, and 100 percent Holy Spirit SIMULTANEOUSLY. So, now you see it, and now you understand it.

*

45. Romans 8:18-23

18 I consider that our present sufferings are not worth comparing with the glory that will be revealed in us. 19 *The creation* waits in eager expectation for the sons of God to be revealed. 20 For *the creation* was subjected to frustration, not by its own choice, but by the will of the one who subjected it, in hope 21 that the creation itself will be liberated from its bondage to decay and brought into the glorious freedom of the children of God.

22 We know that the *whole creation* has been groaning as in the pains of childbirth right up to the present time. 23 Not only so, but we ourselves, who have the first fruits of the Spirit, groan inwardly as we wait eagerly for our adoption as sons, the redemption of our bodies.

I must admit, I am not sure how to comment on this verse of scripture, only to say that in light of the revelation of Romans 1:20 and Genesis 1:1, these verses are extremely interesting. If you have any comments or suggestions, e-mail me at <u>Godisatrinity1@live.com</u>.

46. Romans 8:38-39

38 For I am convinced that neither death nor life, neither angels nor demons, neither the **present** nor the **future**, nor any powers, 39 neither **height** nor **depth**, nor **anything else in all creation**, will be able to separate us from the love of God that is in Christ Jesus our Lord.

Notice that time (present and future), space (height and depth) and matter (anything else in all creation) will NOT be able to separate us from the love of God that is in Christ Jesus our Lord. Only God Himself could make that choice, and time, space, and matter are NOT God (Pantheism is WRONG). Time, space, and matter reflect God's divine nature PERFECTLY, but they are NOT God, any more than a pot (the created) is the same as the potter (the creator).

See also Ephesians 3:18-19.
*

47. Romans 9:5

5 Theirs are the patriarchs, and from them is traced the human ancestry of **Christ, who is God** over all, forever praised! Amen.

This verse is one of the strongest statements that Jesus Christ is 100 percent human AND 100 percent God.
*

48. 2 Corinthians 13:14

14 May the grace of the **Lord Jesus Christ**, and the love of **God**, and the fellowship of the **Holy Spirit** be with you all.

In this verse the divine nature of God is expressed in one verse, with one of the MAJOR FUNCTIONS of each person of the Godhead expressed. GRACE and truth came through Jesus Christ (see John 1:17), God the Father IS love (see 1 John 4:8 & 16) and without His love we would be lost. John 3:16 "For God so loved the world that he gave his one and only Son, that whoever believes in him shall not perish but have eternal life), and Gal 5:22-23 says, "But the fruit of the Spirit is love, joy, peace, patience, kindness, goodness, faithfulness, 23 gentleness and self-control. Against such things there is no law". Without the fruits of the Spirit (which is cultivated through interaction with the Holy Spirit) there would be no **supernatural** love, joy, peace, patience, kindness, goodness, faithfulness, gentleness and self-control to nurture our relationships with Jesus the son, and with the Father. So the Holy Spirit is who makes it possible to have intimate fellowship with the Father, the Son, and each other.
*

49. Ephesians 1:9-10

9 And he made known to us the **mystery of his will** according to his good pleasure, which he purposed in Christ, 10 to be put into effect when **the times will have reached their fulfill-ment**-to bring all things in **heaven** and on **earth** together under one head, even Christ.

Notice that in Genesis 1:1, the beginning of all things reflected time, space and matter, and time, space, and matter are there in Ephesians 1:9-10 which speaks of the fulfillment of all things, and God said in Revelation 22:19 "I am the Alpha and the Omega, the First and the Last, the Beginning and the End."
*

50. Ephesians 3:17-19

17 so that Christ may dwell in your hearts through faith. And I pray that you, being rooted and established in love, 18 may have power, together with all the saints, to grasp how **_WIDE_**

and _**LONG**_ and **HIGH** and _**DEEP**_ is the **love** of Christ, 19 and to **know** this love that surpasses knowledge-that you may be filled to the measure of all the **fullness** of God.

See Job 11:7-9 (the mysteries of God expressed as an area of space).

In this passage of scripture, Christ's love (and _**God IS love**_: see 1 John 4:8) is described in the exact same way one would describe an area of SPACE, that is, as having the three dimensions of width, height, and depth. Notice that there is NO SPACE without all three dimensions (width, height, and depth). If all you have is two dimensions (width and depth for example) you have something you can talk about and write books about, but it is not EXPERIENCABLE until the third dimension is added.

This scripture then, is a marvelous confirmation that what God is like (what His divine nature is like) can be VERY CLEARLY PERCEIVED by observing _**space**_, one of the three "aspects" of the creation. All three aspects were created at the same point in time that the world was created (Genesis 1:1).

See also Psalms 103:11.

*

51. Philippians 2:6-11

6 **Who, being in very nature God**,
did not consider equality with God something to be
grasped,
7 but made himself nothing,
taking the very nature of a servant,
being made in human likeness.
8 And being found in appearance as a man,
he humbled himself
and became obedient to death-
even death on a cross!
9 Therefore God exalted him to the highest place
and gave him the name that is above every name,
10 that at the name of Jesus every knee should bow,

in **heaven** and on **earth** and under the earth,
11 and every tongue confess that Jesus Christ is Lord,
to the glory of God the Father.

If Jesus, the son, is in very nature God, then He "takes on" the divine nature of God explained in Romans 1:20 and Genesis 1:1. Jesus, on the Mount of Transfiguration (see Matthew 17:1-9) showed Peter, James, and John this divine nature in all its GLORY.
*

52. Colossians 1:15-23

15 **He is the image of the invisible God**, the firstborn over all creation. 16 For by him all things **were created**: things in **heaven** and on **earth**, visible and invisible, whether thrones or powers or rulers or authorities; **all things were created by him and for him**. 17 He is before all things, and **in him all things hold together**. 18 And he is the head of the body, the church; he is the beginning and the firstborn from among the dead, so that in everything he might have the supremacy. 19 **For God was pleased to have all his fullness dwell in him**, 20 and through him to reconcile to himself all things, whether things on **earth** or things in **heaven**, by making peace through his blood, shed on the cross.
21 Once you were alienated from God and were enemies in your minds because of your evil behavior. 22 But now he has reconciled you **by Christ's physical body** through death to present you holy in his sight, without blemish and free from accusation-

See also, 2 Corinthians 4:4.
Learning how to explain the Trinity answers one set of questions, but a whole new set of questions arise.
I am going to comment on verse 15 by posing a question: is Jesus a miniature form of God the Father "brought down to size" so us humans can relate to him? Some of you reading this were puzzled when reading Chapter 1 of this book. You NEEDED to read Chapter

3 and have it all "brought down to size" (the puppet stage) so your mind could grasp it. I am absolutely NOT trying to get loony here, but this is the kind of question that comes to my mind when I read that Jesus is the image of the invisible God (the Father). If God the Father's nature can be **understood** by observing space (see Jeremiah 23:24), then God the Father must be unspeakably large (how big is space?), yet Jesus took on human form.

We all can relate to man's fascination with the unspeakably large (space), and the unspeakably small (the electron), and in both of these two extremes, man NEEDED HELP to even <u>begin</u> to understand them (the most powerful telescope, and the most powerful microscope). Well, Jesus came to help us KNOW the Father (see John 1:18). Indeed, who can fathom the mysteries of God (Job 11:7-9)?

Notice that in Christ all things "hold together" (verse 17). Jesus the Son is not only represented by matter in the time/space/matter analogy authorized by Romans 1:20, but Christ also SUSTAINS matter by holding it together.

*

53. Colossians 2:1-3

2 My purpose is that they may be encouraged in heart and united in love, so that they may have the full riches of complete understanding, in order that they may know the mystery of God, namely, **Christ**, in *<u>whom are hidden all the treasures of wisdom and knowledge.</u>*

Millions of well meaning people, Christians and non-Christians alike, have debated the essence of God's divine nature for the last two millennia. The opponents of Christianity have proclaimed the scriptures to be in error. How can the scriptures speak of the Father being God, the Son being God, and the Holy Spirit being God, but yet it says CLEARLY that there is only ONE God? Countless numbers of books have been written by scholarly Christians proving conclusively from scripture that the Father is God, the Son is God, and the Holy Spirit is God, yet there is but one God. So not being able to explain how this can be so, it has been proclaimed a mystery. But, indeed, "all the treasures of wisdom and knowledge are HIDDEN IN CHRIST." God has indeed chosen to reveal the essence of His divine nature, and it is NOT a mystery. For now you "see" it, and now you "understand" it.

If what you just read still doesn't make any sense to you, I suggest you go back and re-read Chapter 1 of this book.

See also Jeremiah 33:2-3.

*

54. Hebrews 1:3

3 **The Son is** the radiance of **God's** glory and *the exact representation of his being*, sustaining all things by his powerful word. After he had provided purification for sins, he sat down at the right hand of the Majesty in heaven.

Some might say that it is erroneous to talk about the PHYSICAL NATURE of God, because God is Spirit (John 4:24). It is true that God is spirit. It is also true that he is a spirit capable of manifesting himself in a seeable form of matter if He so chooses. This was true in the theophanies (physical appearances of God) in the Old Testament, it was true during the thirty-three years that Jesus walked the earth, and it WILL BE true when Jesus comes again to receive His church in glory, for then we shall *see him* as he is (see 1 John 3:2).

On the Mount of Transfiguration (see Matt 17:1-2) it says the following:

17:1 After six days Jesus took with him Peter, James, and John the brother of James, and led them up a high mountain by themselves. 2 There *he was transfigured* before them. His face shone *like the sun*, and his clothes became *as white as the light*.

Hebrews 1:3 suggests that the real "transfiguration" took place thirty-three years earlier in a stable in Bethlehem. Jesus on the "Mount of Transfiguration" was actually seen in his "natural" state.

The scripture says "God is light" (1 John 1:5). As a matter of fact, 1 John 1:5 states that Jesus had told them that all along. Peter, James, and John saw Jesus return to his original GLORY. The glory only God possesses, and the glory born again Christians shall all partake in for all eternity.

*

55. Hebrews 1:10-12

10 He also says,
"In the ***BEGINNING***, O Lord, you laid the foundations of the ***EARTH***,
and the ***HEAVENS*** are the work of your hands.
11 ***They*** will perish, ***but you*** remain;
they will all wear out like a garment.
12 You will roll them up like a robe;
like a garment ***they will be changed***.
But you remain the same,
and your years will never end."

In Psalms 102:25-28 the Psalmist ***CONTRASTS*** time, space, and matter with Yahweh Himself (see scripture No.18 and notes). In Hebrews 1:1 through 1:13 there are seven great proclamations made about the Son, Jesus. In Hebrews 1:10-12, Psalms 102:25-28 is quoted, and applied to the Son, making the Son and Yahweh one and the same.

Our God is a jealous God. He engraved with his own finger the words, "You shall have no other gods before me." (Exodus 20:3), and the scriptures affirm "To who will you COMPARE God? (See Isaiah 40:18). But obviously, the Lord Jesus DOES allow something to be CONTRASTED with him. And that is time, space, and matter.

*

56. Hebrews 9:14

14 How much more, then, will the blood of **Christ**, who through the **eternal Spirit** offered himself unblemished to

God, cleanse our consciences from acts that lead to death, so that we may serve the living God!

Notice that the Son, the Holy Spirit, and the Father all played a key role in bringing salvation to mankind. Without the contribution of each of the three, we would still be living with our sins.
*

57. 2 Peter 3:5-10

5 But they deliberately forget that *long ago* by God's word the **heavens** existed and the **earth** was formed out of water and by water. 6 By these waters also the world of that time was deluged and destroyed. 7 By the same word the *present* **heavens** and **earth** are reserved for fire, being kept for **the day of judgment** and destruction of ungodly men.
8 But do not forget this one thing, dear friends: With the Lord a day is like a thousandyears, and a thousand years are like a day. 9 The Lord is not slow in keeping his promise, as some understand slowness. He is patient with you, not wanting anyone to perish, but everyone to come to repentance. 10 But **the day of the Lord will come** like a thief. The **heavens** will disappear with a roar; **the elements** will be destroyed by fire, and the **earth** and everything in it will be laid bare.

This is an interesting passage. Verse 5 contains time (long ago), space (heavens), and matter **IN THE PAST**. Verse 7 contains time (present), space (heavens), and matter (earth) **IN THE PRESENT**, and Verse 10 contains time (will come), space (heavens), and matter (the elements and earth) **IN THE FUTURE**, and Jesus said, "I am the Alpha and the Omega, the beginning and the end."(See Revelation 22:13).

2 Peter 3:1-13 is the "Day of the Lord" passage, and God's divine nature is intricately woven into the text. Can you "see" it?
*

58. 1 John 2:23

23 No one who denies the Son has the Father; **whoever acknowledges the Son has the Father also.**

Notice again, the fact that the Father and the Son cannot be separated. This makes what happened at the cross even more mind boggling.
*

59. 1 John 2:24-25

24 See that what you have heard from ***the beginning*** remains in you. If it does, you also will remain in the ***Son*** and in the ***Father***. 25 And this is what he promised us-even eternal life.

Notice that this passage describes the path to eternal life with time (the beginning), Son (matter), and Father (space) in its context.

I would suggest that in Verse 24 the Holy Spirit could be substituted for "the beginning" and it would not change the meaning of the scripture. "See that what you have heard from the Holy Spirit remains in you."
*

60. Revelation 22:13

13 I *am* the Alpha and the Omega, the First and the Last, the ***Beginning*** and the ***End.***

What an interesting verse of scripture this is! The Lord here describes himself as the three tenses of time. I AM is the PRESENT tense of time, the BEGINNING is the PAST tense of time, and the END is the FUTURE tense of time, and Jesus says "this is what I AM."

Notice that "in the beginning" **all** time was future, at some point in time **all** time will have been present, and in the end, **all** time will be past.

See also Revelation 1:4-8, 17; 2:8; 4:8; 21:6

*

This completes the Through the Bible "Trinity Study." If any reader sees a scripture he or she believes should be included this Bible Study, PLEASE send me the information at the e-mail address below.

I do not pretend to be a Greek or Hebrew scholar. I do not pretend to have all the answers or the final say in how to explain the Trinity. It occurs to me that seeing how to explain the essence of God's divine nature answers some questions, and opens up a million NEW questions. So if you have questions, comments, or corrections, e-mail me at <u>Godisatrinity1@live.com</u>.

Amen. Come Lord Jesus.

CHAPTER III

HOW TO EXPLAIN THE TRINITY TO YOUR CHILD USING A PUPPET STAGE

This is priceless!

Get a box, perhaps 3' X 3' X 3' square (or any good size box would do), and cut out a big portion of one side (leave the back in tact) making a stage-like appearance. You may paint the box if you wish, but it is not necessary.

For added effect if you wish, hang a ball representing the earth on a string and position it right in the middle of your stage.

Get a good quality one-hand type puppet. Monkey puppets are easy to find and very effective.

Now sit your children (or Children's group) down in front of your puppet stage, and say the following:

"Hey kids, would anyone like to know what God is like?" (I assure you, every hand will go up with enthusiasm).

"Christians believe there is just one God (hold up one finger as you say this for emphasis and clarity), not three Gods, right? (Let the kids answer before proceeding).

"But we also believe God is Father, Son, and Holy Spirit. Does that seem hard to understand? How can there be just one God, but He is Father, Son, and Holy Spirit?"

(Hold up 1, 2, and then 3 fingers as you say this).

"Alright kids, listen real close because I am going to teach you how to explain that to your friends. OK?"

In the Bible, in the book of Romans, chapter 1 and verse 20 it says these words:

"For since the creation of the world God's invisible qualities – His eternal power and divine nature (and that means what God is like) – have been CLEARLY SEEN, being UNDERSTOOD from what has been made, so that men are without excuse.

OK? What that scripture is saying to us is that if we go back to the point in time when the world was created, and that was in the very first verse of the Bible, Genesis 1:1, and look at the things that God used to make His creation, those things should show us something about what God is like.

Now we can't know EVERYTHING about God. All we can know is what God chooses to show us. Right? Well, let's see what God chose to show us here.

Genesis 1:1 says "in the BEGINNING God created the HEAVENS and the EARTH".

There were 3 things that came into existence in that verse, and they were:

1) TIME. "The Beginning" was the beginning of time.
2) SPACE. The word "heavens" is referring to space.
3) MATTER. Matter is stuff you can see. Real stuff. There is also real stuff that you can't see. For example, this air right here (say this while defining an area of space with your hands – with height, width, and depth).

Does anyone think that air is NOT real stuff? Let's see (blow up a balloon and then tap on the balloon). Yep it's real stuff isn't it? It is called gases. Gases in the air.

OK, now how can we find out something about what God is like by looking at time, space, and matter?

Well, let's pretend that **all of God's creation is all inside this puppet stage**. Here are the stars up here (say this pointing to the upper area of your puppet stage), and here is the earth (pointing to the middle of the puppet stage, and here you kids are on the earth (again pointing to the earth, or the middle of the stage).

"Now puppet, see if you can find somewhere in this puppet stage where there isn't any space" (move the puppet around the stage while moving his arms as if "feeling in the air").

Then the puppet says, "Wow, I guess space is EVERYWHERE inside here"! And you say, "That's right. Space is ALL inside this puppet stage. (the word all can be drawn out for emphasis, i.e.

aaaaaalllllll). "Is that right kids?" (They will agree with you most of the time).

Then you say "Now puppet, see if you can find somewhere in this puppet stage where there isn't any air, or light, or stuff you can see. <u>Matter</u> – right?" (Nod your head to acknowledge the truth of this and the kids will agree with you).

The puppet takes a deep breath in all 4 corners, looks up at the earth and the sun and the stars, then looks at his own feet, then says, "Wow, I guess air and light and stuff you can see (matter) is EVERYWHERE in here!"

You say, "That's right!" Air and light and stuff you can see completely FILLS the puppet stage, doesn't it.

Now hand the puppet your watch and say, "Now puppet, see if you can find somewhere in this puppet stage where there isn't any <u>time</u>".

The puppet moves the watch around the puppet stage, looking at the watch as he goes.

The puppet says, "Wow! I guess time is EVERYWHERE inside here!"

You say, "That's right! Time completely fills the puppet stage doesn't it".

So let's review what we just learned. Space AND matter AND time all 3 completely fill the puppet stage. Right? And they all 3 fill the puppet stage ALL AT ONCE.

Well now, that should tell us something about what God is like. Just like what God made is all space, all matter, and all time all at one time, God is all Father, all Son, and all Holy Spirit all at one time. So although there is only one God, He is 100% Father, 100% Son, and 100% Holy Spirit all at once! And now notice that you can't take time out of this puppet stage, you can't take space out of this puppet stage, and you can't take air and light and stuff you can see out of this puppet stage. In other words, time, space, and matter can't be separated from one another. Right? Well, that is what God is like.

Romans 1:20 says we ought to be able to <u>clearly see</u> and we ought to be able to <u>understand</u> what God's divine nature is like. Do you understand it now?

Would you like to explain the Trinity to me now?

If you have questions, comments, or corrections, feel free to e-mail me at <u>Godisatrinity1@live.com</u>

Amen. Come Lord Jesus

CONCLUSION

The critics of the Christian doctrine of the Trinity have been answered. Their claim that the doctrine of the Trinity is illogical and unexplainable has been found untrue. The fact that scholarly Christians during the last two millennia have frequently called the Trinity unexplainable does not logically make their statements true. They simply had incomplete revelation. Indeed there have been "great treasures of wisdom and knowledge HIDDEN in Christ" (Colossians 2:2-3).

If we are authorized in Romans 1:20, to clearly see and understand the essence of God's divine nature by considering what was created in Genesis 1:1, and what was created in Genesis 1:1 is a perfect Trinity of time, space, and matter, then we should approach the scriptures seeking a God whose divine nature is EXACTLY as represented by time, space, and matter. Just like we call the universe the UNI-verse, we should then expect the God of the Bible to be a UNI-God (one God) capable of manifesting Himself in three distinct ways, yet COMPLETELY undividable.

The Trinity is not only true, but according to the Law of Cause and Effect, the God of the Bible, who manifests Himself as Father, Son, and Holy Spirit, is the ONLY logical explanation for the creation of a universe that is a PERFECT TRINITY of time, space, and matter.

The reader of this book now KNOWS their God physically. If you would like to KNOW Him personally, simply turn the page.

It is my hearts cry that these writings will prove to be a monumental blessing to the body of Christ, and an encouragement to those who are honestly seeking to know God.

THE PRAYER FOR SALVATION

Heavenly Father, I know that I have sinned against you and that my sins separate me from you. I am truly sorry. I now want to turn away from my past sinful life, and turn to you for forgiveness. Please forgive me, and help me avoid sinning in the future. I believe that your son, Jesus Christ, died on the cross for my sins, was resurrected from the dead, is alive, and hears my prayer right now. I invite Jesus to become the Lord of my life, and to rule and reign in my heart from this day forward. Right now, please send your Holy Spirit to help me know You, obey You, and to do Your will for the rest of my life. In Jesus' name I pray, Amen.

If you said this prayer and truly believe it in your heart God will not turn you away. The evidence of your sincerity will be a burning desire to read the Bible, and to respond in obedience in seeking to be water- baptized.

Romans 10:9-10
9 That if you **confess** with your mouth, "**Jesus is Lord**," and **believe** in your heart that God **raised him from the dead**, you **will** be saved. 10 For it is with your heart that you believe and are justified, and it is with your mouth that you confess and are saved.

APPENDIX I

24 "SIGNATURE" SCRIPTURES

Genesis 1:1
1:1 In the *beginning* God created the *heavens* and the *earth.*
NIV

Genesis 2:4
4 This is the account of the *heavens* and the *earth when* they were created.
NIV

Exodus 20:11
11 For in *six days* the LORD made the *heavens* and the *earth,* the sea, and all that is in them, but he rested on the seventh day. Therefore the LORD blessed the Sabbath day and made it holy.
NIV

Exodus 31:17
17 It will be a sign between me and the Israelites *forever,* for in *six days* the LORD made the *heavens* and the *earth,* and on the seventh day he abstained from work and rested.'"
NIV

Deuteronomy 4:26
26 I call *heaven* and *earth* as witnesses against you *this day* that you will quickly perish from the land that you are crossing the Jordan to possess. You will not live there long but will certainly be destroyed.
NIV

Deuteronomy 4:39
39 Acknowledge and take to heart *this day* that the LORD *is* God in *heaven* above and on the *earth* below. There is no other.
NIV

Deuteronomy 11:20-21
21 so that *your days* and the *days of your children* may be many in the land that the LORD swore to give your forefathers, *as many as the days* that the *heavens* are above the *earth*.
NIV

Deuteronomy 30:19
19 *This day* I call *heaven* and *earth* as witnesses against you that I have set before you life and death, blessings and curses. Now choose life, so that you and your children may live
NIV

1 Chronicles 29:10-11
10 David praised the LORD in the presence of the whole assembly, saying,
"Praise be to you, O LORD,
God of our father Israel,
from everlasting to everlasting.
11 Yours, O LORD, is the greatness and the power and the glory and the majesty and the splendor,
for everything in *heaven* and *earth* is yours.
NIV

Psalm 102:25-27
25 In the *beginning* you laid the foundations of the *earth*,
and the *heavens* are the work of your hands.
26 They will perish, but you remain;
they will all wear out like a garment.
Like clothing you will change them
and they will be discarded.
27 But you remain the same,
and your years will never end.
NIV

Isaiah 13:13
13 Therefore I will make the *heavens* tremble;
and the *earth* will shake from its place
at the wrath of the LORD Almighty,
in *the day of* his burning anger.
NIV

Isaiah 44:24
24 "This is what the LORD says —
your Redeemer, who formed you in the womb:
I am the LORD,
who *has made* all things (over time),
who alone stretched out the *heavens*,
who spread out the *earth* by myself,
NIV

Isaiah 48:12-13
12 "Listen to me, O Jacob,
Israel, whom I have called:
I am he;
I am the first and I am the last.
13 My own hand laid the foundations of the *earth*,
and my right hand spread out the *heavens*;
when I summon them,
they all stand up together.
NIV

Jeremiah 33:24-26
25 This is what the LORD says: 'If I have not established my *covenant with day and night* and the fixed laws of *heaven* and *earth*, 26 then I will reject the descendants of Jacob and David my servant and will not choose one of his sons to rule over the descendants of Abraham, Isaac and Jacob. For I will restore their fortunes and have compassion on them.'"
NIV

Jeremiah 51:47-48
47 For *the time* will surely come
when I will punish the idols of Babylon;
her whole land will be disgraced
and her slain will all lie fallen within her.
48 Then *heaven* and *earth* and all that is in them
will shout for joy over Babylon,
for out of the north
destroyers will attack her,"
declares the LORD.
NIV

Daniel 6:25-28
25 Then King Darius wrote to all the peoples, nations and men of every language throughout the land:
"May you prosper greatly!
26 "I issue a decree that in every part of my kingdom people must fear and reverence the God of Daniel.
"For he is the living God
and he *endures forever*;
his kingdom will not be destroyed,
his dominion will *never end*.
27 He rescues and he saves;
he performs signs and wonders
in the *heavens* and on the *earth*.
He has rescued Daniel
from the power of the lions."

28 So Daniel prospered during the reign of Darius and the reign of Cyrus the Persian.
NIV

Joel 2:28-32
28 'And afterward,
I will pour out my Spirit on all people.
Your sons and daughters will prophesy,
your old men will dream dreams,
your young men will see visions.
29 Even on my servants, both men and women,
I will pour out my Spirit *in those days*.
30 I will show wonders in the *heavens*
and on the *earth*,
blood and fire and billows of smoke.
31 The sun will be turned to darkness
and the moon to blood
before the coming of the great and dreadful *day of the LORD*.
32 And everyone who calls
on the name of the LORD will be saved;
for on Mount Zion and in Jerusalem
there will be deliverance,
as the LORD has said,
among the survivors
whom the LORD calls.
NIV

Haggai 2:6-9
6 "This is what the LORD Almighty says: 'In *a little while* I will once more shake the *heavens* and the *earth*, the sea and the dry land. 7 I will shake all nations, and the desired of all nations will come, and I will fill this house with glory,' says the LORD Almighty. 8 'The silver is mine and the gold is mine,' declares the LORD Almighty. 9 'The glory of this present house will be greater than the glory of the former

house,' says the LORD Almighty. 'And in this place I will grant peace,' declares the LORD Almighty."
NIV

Matthew 5:18
18 I tell you the truth, _until_ (up to the time that) _heaven_ and _earth_ disappear, not the smallest letter, not the least stroke of a pen, will by any means disappear from the Law until everything is accomplished.
NIV

Mark 13:26-27
26 "_At that time_ men will see the Son of Man coming in clouds with great power and glory. 27 And he will send his angels and gather his elect from the four winds, from the ends of the _earth_ to the ends of the _heavens_
NIV

Luke 10:21
21 At _that time Jesus_, full of joy through the _Holy Spirit_, said, "I praise you, _Father_, Lord of _heaven_ and _earth_, because you have hidden these things from the wise and learned, and revealed them to little children. Yes, Father, for this was your good pleasure.
NIV

Ephesians 1:9-10
9 And he made known to us the mystery of his will according to his good pleasure, which he purposed in Christ, 10 to be put into effect _when the times_ will have reached their fulfill-ment-to bring all things in _heaven_ and on _earth_ together under one head, even Christ.
NIV

Hebrews 1:10-12
10 He also says,
"In the *beginning*, O Lord, you laid the foundations of the *earth*,
and the *heavens* are the work of your hands.
11 They will perish, but you remain;
they will all wear out like a garment.
12 You will roll them up like a robe;
like a garment they will be changed.
But you remain the same,
and your years will never end."
NIV

Revelation 14:7
7 He said in a loud voice, "Fear God and give him glory, because *the hour of his judgment* has come. Worship him who made the *heavens*, the *earth*, the sea and the springs of water."
NIV

APENDIX II

TIME / HOLY SPIRIT, SPACE / FATHER, MATTER / SON in the New Testament.

MATTHEW

4:17	Time	Son	Space
5:18	Time	Matter	Space
11:25	Time	Son	Father
12:28	Spirit	Son	Father
24:30	Time	Son	Space
28:19	Spirit	Son	Father

MARK

1:1	Time (beginning)	Son	Father
1:10	Spirit	Son	Space
13:26-27	Time (time)	Matter (earth)	Space (heavens)
13:32	Time (time)	Son	Father/Space

LUKE

1:35	Spirit	Son	Father
2:26	Spirit	Son	Father
3:21-22	Spirit	Son	Father/Space
4:18a	Spirit	Son	Father
9:51	Time (time)	Son	Space (heaven)
10:21	Spirit/Time	Son/Matter	Father/Space
12:56	Time (time)	Matter (earth)	Space(sky)
24:49	Spirit	Son	Father

JOHN

1:1	Time (beginning)	Son	Father
1:2	Time (beginning)	Son	Father
1:32	Spirit	Son	Space
3:34	Spirit	Son	Father
6:40	Time (last day)	Son	Father
6:44	Time (last day)	Son	Father
13:1	Time (time)	Son	Father
14:16	Spirit	Son	Father
14:26	Spirit	Son	Father
15:26	Spirit	Son	Father

ACTS

1:1-2	Spirit/time	Son	space (heaven)
1:7-8	Spirit/time	Son	Father
2:1-2	Spirit/day	Matter (house)	Space (heaven)
2:33	Spirit	Son	Father
3:19	Time (times)	Son	Father/space

4:24-25	Spirit	Son/matter	Space (heaven)
7:55	Spirit	Son	Father/space
10:38	Spirit	Son	Father

ROMANS

1:4	Spirit	Son	Father
1:9-10	Time(all times)	Son	Father

1 CORINTHIANS

12:4-6	Spirit	Son	Father
15:24	Time (the end)	Son	Father

2 CORINTHIANS

1:21	Spirit	Son	Father
2:13-14	Spirit	Son	Father

GALATIANS

4:4	Spirit/time	Son	Father

EPHESIANS

1:17	Spirit	Son	Father
2:18	Spirit	Son	Father
2:22	Spirit	Son	Father
3:16	Spirit	Son	Father

1 TIMOTHY

| 2:5-6 | Time (proper time) | Son | Father |
| 6:14-15 | Time (God's own time) | Son | Father |

HEBREWS

1:1-2	Time (many times)	Son	Father
1:10	Time (beginning)	Matter (earth)	Space (heavens)
9:14	Spirit	Son	Father
10:12	Time (all time)	Son (priest)	Father

1 PETER

| 1:2 | Spirit | Son | Father |

1 JOHN

1:1-2	Time (beginning)	Son	Father
2:24	Time (beginning)	Son	Father
4:13-14	Spirit	Son	Father

REVELATION

| 11:15 | Time (forever…..) | Son | Father |